Meadow
of
Whispers

Hannah Mukhtar

979-8-218-23826-1

DEDICATION

Thank you to my friends, family, teachers, and of course, my favorite Spotify Playlist.

ACKNOWLEDGMENTS

I owe a gratitude-filled shoutout to Bhargavi and Dania for their invaluable role in shaping the formatting and editing of my book. They've endured my endless stream of questions and served as the brave souls who first laid eyes on my manuscript. Your input and support have been like a poetic salve to my writer's soul.

And to Mrs. Lauren Drescher, my extraordinary English teacher, thank you for reigniting my interest in poetry. Our daily poems have been a catalyst for my creative growth, pushing me to uncover my unique poetic voice. Your guidance and encouragement have been as vital as metaphors in a poem, propelling me through the poetic odyssey of this book.

CONTENTS

Preface

It's finally here! I'm thrilled to present to you the culmination of a year's worth of effort and growth in poetry. This collection is a blend of my deepest emotions, personal experiences, and thoughts, accompanied by a touch of fantasy (especially in Amor's Garden!).

After noticing a striking resemblance between many of my poems and the symbolism of flowers, which has been interpreted since the Victorian ages, I decided to merge my poetry with photographs of these meaningful blooms. I also have a fondness for aesthetically pleasing books, so I felt compelled to transform my creation into a vision that I, as well as my readers, could truly appreciate. And I must say, it doesn't disappoint. I obtained flower photographs from some of my favorite photographers and edited them to match my desired style. The end result is this book, now resting in your hands, ready to be enjoyed.

My collection doesn't revolve around a single healing theme or message. Instead, it branches out from various thoughts and feelings of mine, much like the branches of a tree. As a teenager, this rings true for me more than ever. My thoughts rarely confine themselves to a single theme; the same goes for my poems. While I can't claim to capture the entirety of the teenage experience (that would require an infinitely long book), I do hope to give a voice to the many teenagers who have shared similar thoughts and experiences as mine.

My journey with poetry has been anything but conventional. Just over a year ago, I discovered my love for poetry when I wrote "Oh so young" for a class project. In the months that followed, I often lacked inspiration and only produced a few poems, overly focused on the results rather than my own progress. However, everything changed when I started writing daily poems with my 11th-grade English teacher. It was then that I truly found my poetic voice.

"Meadow of Whispers" is truly a book of growth, exploring the essence of being a teenager. It captures the unique experiences and emotions of adolescence while incorporating the symbolism of flowers. I wish you a delightful reading experience!

Sincerely,

Floral
Reverie

Introspection

CONTENTS

PETALS

men never have to think about flowers.
the touch, the feel, the need to appease
the innocence of the petal's crease
whether the petal rips
in the moonlight with ease
will bouquets be brought with lilac breeze?
or perhaps roses just to get a tease
the want for petals, the insatiable need
the need for attention from the crowd
the need to continually be proud
the need to be heard aloud but not too loud
men never have to think about flowers.
they never know the want for the crimson petals;
the smell of a lush rose
the crush of petals in one's hands
to be strong and still terrified
innocent and preserved
men never have to think about flowers.

Credit: Bud Jenkins/Pexels

Chrysanthemums embody contradiction in their very essence. With their intricate layers of petals and contrasting colors, they exude both strength and fragility. These flowers hold dual meanings, symbolizing both death and mourning, as well as celebration and joy. Their ability to gracefully reconcile opposing qualities serves as a poignant reminder that contradictions can coexist harmoniously and that beauty can arise from embracing life's paradoxes.

SLEEPLESS LAMENT

It's 3 A.M.,
But my eyes are wide open.
Straining in the dark,
My day appears right before my eyes.

An early morning stretch,
yawning, as I crawl out of bed.
Glancing at myself in the mirror
over-analyzing every dress.

Every action I took at school,
Every mistake I made in turn,
I think and I think
Thinking so much that it hurts again.

What could I have said?
What should I have done?
Questions linger in my mind
as the night silently hums.

It's 4 A.M.,
But my eyes are wide open.
Regrets dance before my eyes.
It's a sleepless tango with my past.

Forget-me-nots carry a poignant symbolism of regrets and overanalyzing, steeped in their name and rich folklore. These delicate blue flowers, with their clusters of tiny blossoms, serve as gentle reminders of past actions and opportunities missed, invoking a wistful longing. Their very name bears a heartfelt plea to be remembered, hinting at the tendency to dwell on past mistakes and engage in overanalysis.

NOSTALGIC

on these summer nights my mind does wander
of summers past in the moonlight haze
more than a decade ago

silly bandz slung around my wrists
blowing bubbles in simple bliss
'twas the brightest of days

water-gun fights in the backyard
sharing secrets and pokémon cards
passing hours in pure delight

in the summer's heat
i built forts in make-believe woods
to keep in safe shade
sprinkling "pixie dust" just for fun

sleepy hollows take me under
gnarly roots scrape over
take me back into those woods
where i can dwell, a child forever

Credit: Mister do/vecteezy.com

Moonflowers embody magical nostalgia with their captivating characteristics and enchanting blooming behavior. These delicate white flowers hold a mesmerizing quality as they unfurl under the moonlight, transporting us to a realm of wonder and enchantment. Their subtle fragrance and radiant glow evoke a profound sense of longing, reminiscent of moonlit nights and romantic escapades. Moonflowers weave cherished memories into our present and immerse us in a nostalgic journey that sparks the imagination.

THE MONARCH

I awaken my eyes
Two dozen shadowed blobs afront
Then I reach for the skies

Kept in a shadowed cage, there she lies
Wrapped in a chrysalis of my own kind
I awaken my eyes

And then a week or two later I arise
Push, push, push and I am out
Then I reach for the skies

The *kids* scream of butterflies
What are they? They release me from the cage
I awaken my eyes

I have traveled to the warmth, the monarchs fantasize
Deep orange wings rest upon a tree
the next generation is here and I am not to be
I awaken my eyes
Then I reach for the skies

Credit: Buddhika Damith/Pexels

Milkweeds hold a special symbolism for monarchs as they play a vital role in the life cycle of these majestic butterflies. Serving as a nurturing host plant, milkweeds provide essential nourishment and a safe haven for monarch butterfly larvae. This unique relationship between milkweeds and monarchs represents the interconnectedness and resilience found in nature. The milkweed's significance as a lifeline for monarchs showcases the balance and transformative journey that monarchs undertake.

BUTTERFLY

butterfly
butter-fly
A crying pot of melted butter
luscious, smooth
creamy as the silky wind

A fly buzzing around my room
zzzzzzzzzzzzz
it goes
annoyingly sauntering about

splashed together
the words clash
oh so beautifully
bright wings upon a willow branch
like a melody
zzzzzzzz
butterfly
oh butter-fly

Credit: Hiểu Hoàng/Pexels

Lotuses hold a deep symbolism of harmony, embodying both grace and resilience. Despite growing in murky waters, they remain untainted, representing the ability to maintain purity amidst challenging circumstances. The gradual unfolding of lotus petals mirrors the journey towards inner peace and enlightenment, as each layer reveals deeper levels of understanding. As a powerful symbol of unity and serenity, lotuses inspire us to find harmony within ourselves and embrace the world around us with a tranquil spirit.

PETUNIA

Oh petunia, petunia
How you wear me dry
Your cries are a menace
Your resentment far worse

Fantasies circle the room
Dancing in the whites of your eyes
The starlit dream of promise
Crushed by your despise

Oh petunia, petunia
I plead with you this time
Wait!
Stay in this box
Just a while
Let me grab those tears in your eyes

Oh petunia, petunia
I know you're scared
Cry waterfalls, till it drains out beneath
Crack drywall with fists of fright
Scribble curses in your journal
Grasp the earth till you stumble
But don't-
Oh no you don't!
Let anyone inside

Petunias embody the essence of anger through their striking and vibrant colors, such as deep reds and fiery oranges. These bold hues evoke a strong sense of passion and intensity, reflecting the raw emotions associated with anger. The resilience and robustness of petunias further underscore the powerful and sometimes overwhelming nature of this emotion. Their presence serves as a visual reminder of the intense energy and potentially destructive force that anger can unleash.

BOO, BOOMBOX

i want to live in an 80s movie
to be at such ease
straightforward signs and feelings
not thinking twice with every action, every tease

only in an 80s movie will there be a sight
of a boombox in one's hand and devotion aflight
does a soundtrack play at the heights of surprise
does the whole world stop for you day and night
does love exist without tragedy or fight

pumping a fist in the air
after winning love
hoist a boombox in one hand
and your heart in the other

that's the only way
you'd ever see me
living life as though-
i were in my favorite 80s movie

Credit: Artem Saranin/Pexels

Red roses embody the essence of simple cinematic love, evoking timeless associations with romance and passion. These iconic flowers, with their velvety petals and alluring fragrance, transport us to the world of classic love stories depicted on the silver screen. Like scenes from a beloved film, red roses symbolize a captivating love that transcends time, capturing the essence of romance in its most enchanting form.

MANGO

a rich, succulent amber
or perhaps a luscious golden hue
slippery as a sip of dew
shiny silhouette of a sunny gem

tangy and tantalizing
but oh so sweet
it takes me back there
in the nighttime heat

out on the porch
slicing through the golden whims
we sat there for hours
just being kids

the taste of childhood
when biting around this fibrous pit
the familiar taste of home
when soaking in the delicious bliss

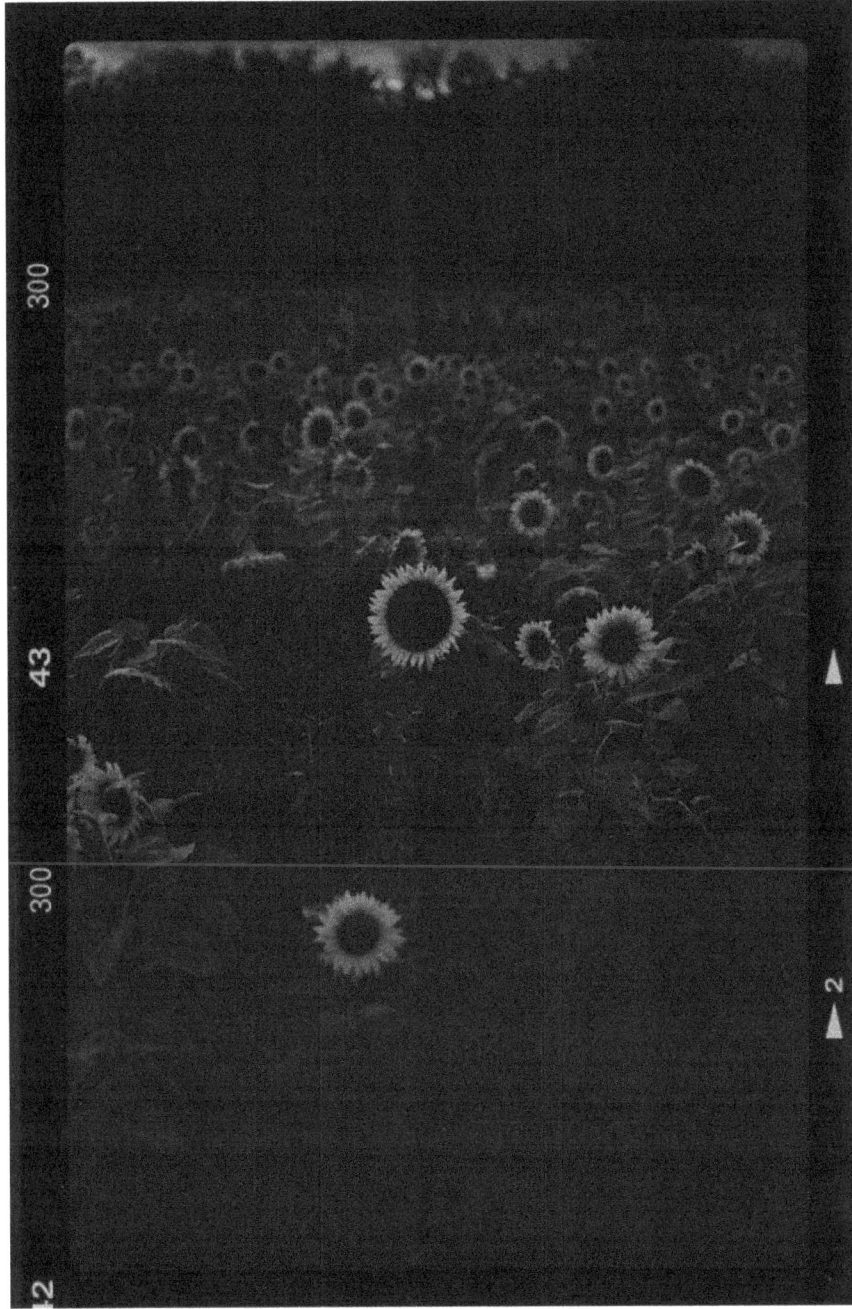

Credit: lil artsy/Pexels

Sunflowers symbolize warmth and childhood with their vibrant presence and joyful connotations. The radiant yellow petals of sunflowers evoke feelings of happiness and the comforting embrace of sunshine. Standing tall on their sturdy stems, their expansive faces embody the spirit of youthful wonder and innocence. Sunflowers hold a nostalgic power, reminding us of carefree days, outdoor escapades, and the simple delights of childhood.

Thorns & Petals

Social Commentary

CONTENTS

SCRAM SUNNY

Light rays peek out behind a cloud
Dumb, old faithful yellow
Get away from my rainy shroud!

Your disposition scares me cowed
I'll hide away in my cynical cave
Until the sunbeam glee is but a cloud

They laughed and giggled loud
Behind silent shades
Until I was backed into-my rainy shroud

I don't need your lemonade crowd
Or your beachy blues
Drift forward, oh onlooking cloud

That's right, thundercloud
Come right this way
Wish upon a stormy cloud
Ever tucked into my rainy shroud

Credit: Yugank Kulshrestha/Pexels

Marigolds embody warmth and optimism through their vibrant colors and infectious cheerfulness. The radiant hues of orange and yellow exude a sunny disposition, spreading positivity and a sense of well-being. Known for their ability to thrive in diverse conditions, marigolds symbolize resilience and a hopeful outlook, serving as a reminder to embrace life's challenges with unwavering optimism. Their lively and uplifting presence inspires us to appreciate the beauty of each day, just as the sun.

BRUSH IT OFF

Shatter the hourglass's grip
Swing with unbridled force
Let the book slam down
-defiantly-

Splinter its fragile frame
Its grains of sand
-smaller than specks-
Weep over the velvet tapestry

And just like that
Time slips away
Minutes, hours, years,
Decades
-centuries-

Endless actions persist
Birth, learning, procreation, death
-just like that-
Life fades into an abyss

So I'll shatter that hourglass
Shards of glass and scattered sands
-time may be lost-
But eternally we'll lay.

Credit: zoosnow/Pexels

Orchids gracefully symbolize the passage of time with their distinctive qualities and unhurried growth. These exquisite flowers possess a long lifespan, slowly blooming and fading away, reminding us of the ephemeral nature of beauty and the ever-changing tides of time. Their delicate elegance serves as a gentle reminder to embrace each precious moment as time quietly carries us forward, leaving behind cherished memories and transformative experiences.

RED

the failure
thick red lines litter the page
they flit and jeer
peering up at me with a menacing glare

a failure
marked like cattle in the slaughter
a letter stands alone in the sea
staring so innocently

my failure
regally sitting upon its throne
of x's and scribbles
the letter stands cruel

these failures
mass manipulator of our kind
pitiful glances turn to dismissive glares
mistakes aren't allowed, didn't you hear?

those failures
line by line
they stack up
a ladder to my mind, sturdy and robust

I'm failure
the red spreads throughout the page
Slowly dripping onto me
until I too am red.
Failure.

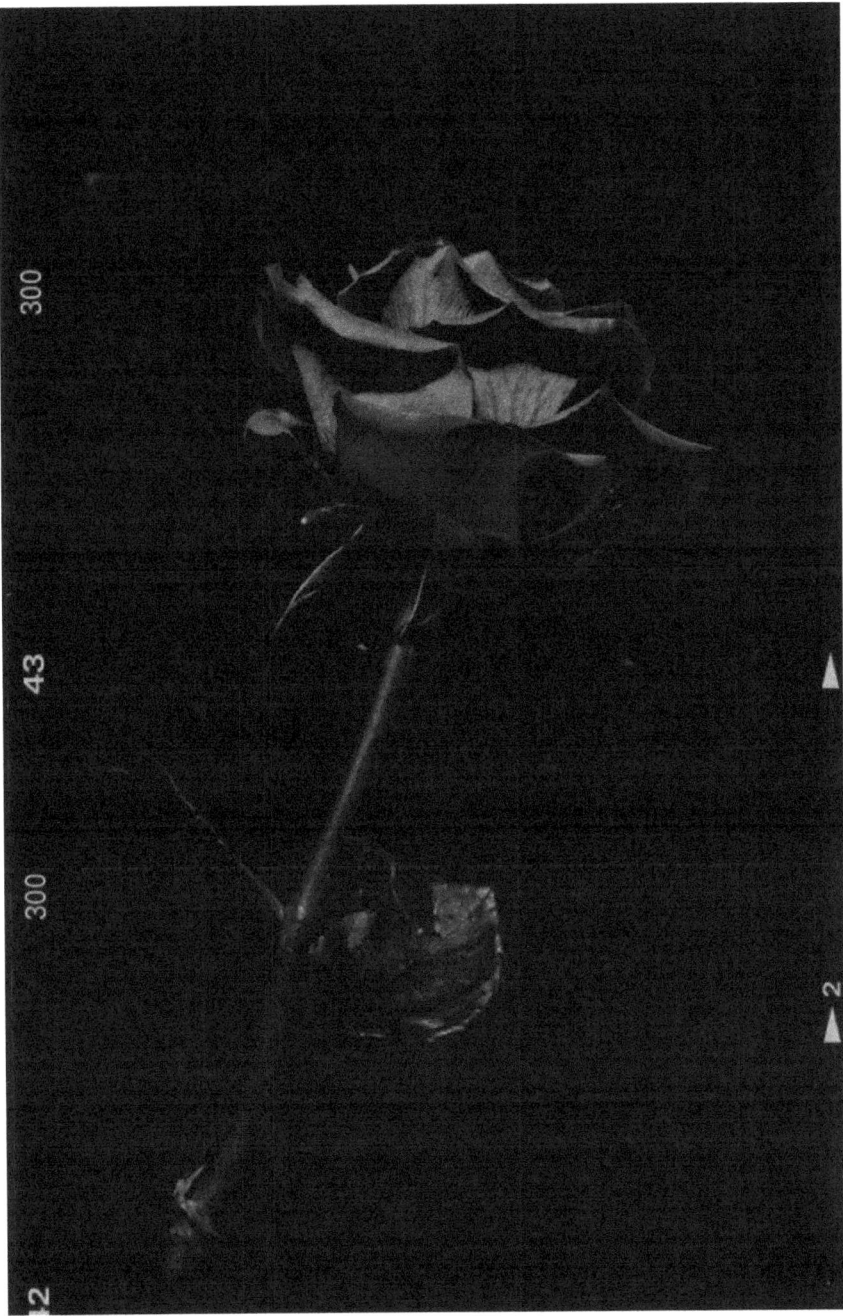

Credit: Adrian Regeci/Pexels

Black roses embody darker emotions and failure through their unconventional color and the emotions they evoke. The deep black hue of these roses signifies mourning, grief, and the somber aspects of human experience. Symbolizing the end of a chapter or unfulfilled expectations, black roses serve as a poignant reminder of setbacks, disappointments, and the complexities of life. Their presence carries a message about embracing the lessons learned from failure and finding strength in the face of adversity.

MISMATCHED

Yes I'm Whitewashed
with a capital W
There's no question
From the tips of my air forces
to the wisps of my burgundy-streaked hair

Yes I'm Whitewashed
When I cover my food
So onlookers don't remark on its smell
When I secretly love it
but I'd never tell

Yes I'm Whitewashed
I'll splurge on "cool hits"
indie and alt-rock on Spotify
But cradle *desi* songs on youtube
at the emotional downs

Yes I'm Whitewashed
That's sure enough
Hiding to evade the constant labels
of being a loser and strange

Yes I'm Whitewashed
But my roots remain strong
In this world of complexities
I find where I belong

Credit: Dominykas/Pexels

Hybrid tea roses embody the essence of cultural blending through their distinctive qualities. With their captivating blooms that gracefully blend different colors, these roses symbolize the beauty that arises when diverse elements come together harmoniously. They represent the celebration of diversity and the recognition of the exquisite beauty that emerges when different cultures intertwine, enriching our society with a vibrant tapestry of unity.

THE CRY HEARD AROUND THE WORLD

Rough white foam brushes up from a wave
reaching for the azure skies
"Woe is mine" she cries

Plastered thick is the grey smoke of the skies
wafting from grouped buildings nearby
They start to chime
the gentle tick-tock of the work time

Serene blue washes up to the shores
swish-swash about
dragging thick green kelp throughout
Green rough and thick
but kelp it was not

Dragged along with sorrowful slump was a grocery bag
twisted around the sea
choking its life and breeze
Oh so gently
humanity creates its disease

Credit: Kubra Kısa/Pexels

Water lilies embody resilience as they gracefully navigate challenging environments. Rising above the muddy waters in which they grow, these exquisite flowers showcase their delicate beauty and unwavering strength. Their ability to bloom and flourish amidst adversity serves as an inspiring symbol of resilience and tenacity. Water lilies remind us to find strength within ourselves, persevere through life's obstacles, and embrace the beauty that can emerge even in the most challenging circumstances.

SILENT HARVEST

Drains her teardrops through a sieve
Watching it descend
Drip by drip
Into the sink beneath
Small glistening jewels left behind
in its wake
She cries a bit more
Till she's drained
Collecting the jewels
in a silk sleeve
she cries out her worth
And harvests her pain.

Credit: Cindy Gustafson/Pexels

Lilies embody inner strength with their graceful presence and unwavering endurance. Standing tall with their elegant blossoms, lilies symbolize resilience and the ability to overcome adversity. They serve as a powerful reminder that true strength originates from within. We should draw upon these inner reserves of strength in order to persevere with grace and resilience, no matter the obstacles we may encounter.

HOLLYWOOD

starlight sprinkles
'cross the quilted ink sky
street signs flash
before my starstruck eyes

dotted crosslights
swerve and dart the evening light
patchy lemon crisscrosses
blare crisp in the cool night

cars dot the rough asphalt
rolling in from the endless dusk
and there you stood
beside palms in a hush

i run- no, i sprint your way
arms open, ready to embrace
i fall into your comforting wrap
of searing contagious fame

stars cascade from above
a shooting star now burns alight
california dreamin'
on such a shattered night

Credit: Noel Ross/Pexels

California poppies symbolize hope for the future with their vibrant and resilient nature. Bursting with bright orange and golden petals, these cheerful flowers represent optimism and a positive outlook. As they bloom abundantly across California's landscapes, they serve as a symbol of renewal and new beginnings, inspiring us to embrace change and cultivate optimism. California poppies remind us of the enduring power of hope and encourage us to pursue our dreams with unwavering determination.

Amor's
Garden

Love

CONTENTS

FLUFFY WINGS

Cupid's arrow just narrowly misses———->- <3
Wedges in a stocky tree
of soft, wafty jasmine

Cupid strikes again
Notches that arrow
And aims straight for my heart———->- <3

Dear you've struck again
But I'll stay here
My heart yearns, but my mind won't listen

A chord chimes in my brain———->- <3
An arrow lodged from the side
Now I'm running-straight into those fluffed wings

An arrow whizzes
Another dozen or so———->- <3
I lie there bleeding, for you I'm sure

Exhausted and languid
Wings float onward to another
And then I realize-
It was all just a game————>

Credit: Greta Hoffman/Pexels

Jasmines are a symbol of love and romance, captivating hearts with their delicate beauty and enchanting fragrance. These exquisite flowers have long been intertwined with affectionate gestures and acts of love. Their intoxicating scent and elegant blooms evoke feelings of passion, sensuality, and romance, creating an ambiance that stirs the depths of the heart. Jasmines hold a cherished place as a symbol of affection and add an element of enchantment to expressions of love.

GINGERLY

It's funny how weather can bring back memories
The sharp cry of a breeze
Sorrow likes to tease
With gentle little drops of river
I touch the sky
Tiptoes in the quiet winding trees
May jerks to December
Lonely days
Cry myself to sleep
Sugar isn't sweeter
than the sweetness of my tears
Holly berries crushed in thy palm
I laugh as the sweet poison reaches
Through my veins, through my heart
I slump my life into your arms
You saved me once
You saved me twice
And now I gladly fall beneath the cracking ice
Crying sugar of iced tea, gingerly

Credit: Eugenia/Pexels

Lilies of the Valley are associated with sincerity and happiness due to their delicate blooms and sweet fragrance, evoking feelings of joy and purity. However, their charm conceals a hidden toxicity, serving as a cautionary reminder of the dualities in nature. The paradoxical nature of the lilies of the valley reflects the intricate complexities of life, reminding us to be mindful of the potential risks that can accompany beauty.

GREY

Trace the lines of your palm
Front and back
The little etchings curl and swirl
Branch and whirl

Count till a hundred
The figures blur
You take a step
Fast forward

I walk in a circle
till my heels ache
Trip in a puddle
and fall into a wilted bloom lake

Pluck the lily petals off
one by one
Arrange it in a circlet
upon your gray head

Crave these idle doings
to let time pass
I brush the circlet off your tomb
And leave you to rest.

Credit: Thomas Plets/Pexels

Cactus flowers embody endurance and unconditional love as they bloom amidst the harshness of the desert, symbolizing the strength to overcome adversity and thrive in challenging circumstances. The prickly nature of cacti reflects the protective and unconditional love that can exist, as they guard their delicate flowers with sharp spines, reminding us of the unwavering care and devotion that transcends obstacles and challenges.

AND THEN IT STARTED POURING

Sky of azure, clear as pools
As the water of the deep, deep blue
But in her dreams
The glistening slick with the tears of a fallen canoe

Striped with glum was the sky above
Shades of smoky gunmetal gray
Then with hues ultramarine and sky blues
Cloudy, thundery horsemen of spray

I whispered to the gray skies, "Come home, you know you're
missed."
down the murmurs came in sparkling dots of crystal tears
And down it came, it ran and ran
My face now plastered with rainy drizzle smears

"Thud, thud, thud" the silky sound of sky's delight
Scents of earthy ichor waft
And watery pails spill over the lands
It brings me back softly, oh so oft

Your eyes were soft as summer rain
Softly gliding down your skin
Giggling as we stomped in puddles
Falling headfirst with a grin

Soppy thick tears edge down my cheek
Like a snail, creep, creep, creep
Salty tears and a watery rush
The "I miss you's" I whisper in my sleep

Your fingers snap like twigs on a branch
Beckoning, calling me forth
My heart jerks each time your voice is in the wind
You break it in half and leave me to the earth

Only on a rainy day, it happens so
One whiff of a drop, and I'll be home
Right back to that rainy, sorrowful day
And now you drift among the seafoam.

Credit: Tibor Szabo/Pexels

Irises embody hope and cherished memories through their graceful elegance and vibrant colors, inspiring us to hold onto hope even in the face of adversity. With their delicate blooms, ranging from soft pastels to bold hues, irises capture the fleeting moments that become cherished memories. They serve as a gentle reminder to appreciate the beauty of the present while treasuring the memories that have shaped our lives, filling our hearts with hope and gratitude.

<u>HOURGLASS</u>

take a dive with me
deeper than the currents
deep under the sea

as sleepy waves
collide and crash
let us watch them from beneath

bubbles as the breeze
it brushes over my skin
so cozy and dear to me

let it envelop us in its soft embrace
and the sand be just below
to sink your feet

let's build a home
in this beautiful and cruel sea
forever still in time
and you're still here with me

Credit: Sheng-lu Wu/Pexels

Heliotropes are powerful symbols of eternal love, captivating us with their intoxicating fragrance and rich symbolism. These flowers have been revered for centuries as emblems of unwavering devotion and everlasting affection. The name "heliotrope" itself, derived from the Greek words for "sun" and "turn," beautifully captures their characteristic of turning to face the sun, representing the enduring nature of love's pursuit of warmth and light.

MAGNETS

opposites attract they say
you were the thundery rain
breaking into a cool night
i was the fool-hearted sun
a bright sunflower gone aflight

two boats passing through the night
one made a wrong turn
we crashed and burned
till something new formed

a little uncertain
a little abrupt
but nonetheless, it was us
i could change you, i knew i could
love has no limits, that's what they say

but life isn't a love song
the rain kept pouring and pouring
flooding the sunflower till it died
alone and drowned

crumpled on the floor i cried
you broke me to pieces
and never bothered to fix me
opposites attract i say
but in the end- we pushed each other away

Credit: Debendra Das/Pexels

Tuberoses carry the symbolic weight of dangerous love, emanating an enchanting fragrance and displaying a captivating beauty. These flowers possess a scent that is both mesmerizing and overwhelming, mirroring the allure and risks that come with intense passion. The delicate purity of their white blooms stands in contrast to the potent aroma they release, serving as a reminder of the intricate and complex nature of love.

<u>DAHLIA ADIEU</u>

Roll a dice
take a stumble
Cry a lake
watch you mumble

Drag a sunflower
across the spring's breeze
Till it crumples
in summer's heat

I gather my things
-a scrap of lace
-a gold-dipped watch
-a velvet glove
-an orange creamsicle
and toss it in the lake
Frost cuts the sun
and you still aren't back

I toss the rest in the lake
and wait for a glimmer or even a murmur
Dahlias blow in the wind and still-
Silence

Credit: Debendra Das/Pexels

Dahlias embody the essence of devoted love with their breathtaking beauty and vibrant hues. These flowers carry a profound symbolism, representing the depth of emotions and unwavering commitment in matters of the heart. With their intricate layers of petals, dahlias serve as a visual metaphor for the complexities and layers of love's devotion.

Serenity's Blossom

Blossom

Reflections

CONTENTS

THE DIG

(TW: Eating Disorder)

dig.dig.find.
the feelings of disgust creep by
i think it'd better if i were blind.

gentle tip taps remind
the perfect person walks past
dig.dig.find.

all angles, no curves defined
happy, pretty eyes dead and hazed.
i think it better if i were blind.

and so i did the reasonable grind.
i starved myself night and day, in every way
dig.dig.find.

a skeleton comes across the wind.
beautiful and thin, gleaming white and free.
i think it better if i were blind.

i need more, so i refined.
miles of workouts keep me on track.
dig.dig.find.

a rotten apple core creeps behind
i kick it, and it rolls away.
i think it better if I were blind.

a torn moth wing comes declined.
i rip it more and it flies away.
dig.dig.find.

the hole is now outlined.
i take a step back and plunge in.
dig.dig.find.
i think it better if i were blind.

Credit: Olga Divnaya/Pexels

Black-eyed susans symbolize a powerful symbol of encouragement and resilience, evident in their radiant yellow petals and contrasting dark centers. These resilient flowers possess a remarkable ability to thrive amidst challenging circumstances, serving as a testament to the human spirit's capacity to persevere. The vivid juxtaposition between their vibrant petals and the darkness at their core signifies the delicate balance between optimism and acknowledging the hardships we face.

OH SO YOUNG

(TW: Eating Disorder)

Oh so young and oh so innocent
what the future held, oh so distant

my body was changing in many ways
but i still wanted to follow in on the latest craze

we were all in a circle in 6th grade
and it was in this very conversation that i had strayed

the girl pointed out everyone's skinniness
then paused on me and said i was an average weight, making me
doubt my own prettiness

why is my body different from theirs i had thought
whilst I hatched a plan to make it not

searching up on YouTube the different ways to lose weight
all of this began to seem like fate

at first it was cutting out junk food and a little exercise
It was all worth it to be the right size

my parents' warnings were left unheard
because their talks of me already being beautiful seemed absurd

then it was smaller portions and a little more exercise
i thought it was all worth it if i could get thinner thighs

frequent visits to the weighing scales,
even gaining a fraction of a pound would mean I had failed

even though my body and weight were healthy
i was still set on viewing them as my enemy

even after losing a significant amount of weight
my reflection was still a sight I learned to hate

my time was solely spent with the weighing scale

not with family, nor with friends
next to it everything else seemed to pale

soon it was down to skipping meals,
purposefully being late to breakfast so i could fit my ideals

my health was steadily getting worse,
but my weight still seemed like the only curse

every little bit of exercise soon consumed my day
every waking moment not in a gym, i obsessed over the weigh

the little food that I ate gave me no energy,
simply a facade to hide my lethargy

i sought the validation of others, but there was none to find
you see, i was atypical even amongst my own kind

my happiest day back then was when a woman called me a little thin
not when I got a good grade on my test
not when I hung out with my best friend
not even my birthday

but it wasn't obvious that I had an issue
because my outside appearance was no cause for a tissue

my parents had taken me to a doctor, fearing my weight loss
hoping that she could make the message come across

the doctor said that i was still at a healthy weight,
making me so upset, that her message didn't come straight

every time someone didn't say hi to me,
i thought my so-called fatness was to blame,
so all i felt was sadness and shame

I used certain apps to track the food I ate,
The numbers only seemed to motivate

my little joys came from the pounds i had shed
so much that i didn't notice my body growing tired

my hair falling in clumps
dizziness which didn't leave me with dread

but i still continued on like that, only growing worse
my eating and exercise getting further adverse

I'm not sure when or why things began to change
but after months of torture, i began to nurture my body again, how
strange

The hurt began to flow away
My harmful habits kept at bay

Oh so young and oh so innocent
wow she feels oh so distant

Credit: Rov Camato/Pexels

Daisies carry a symbolic representation of innocence through their unpretentious and delightful presence. With their white petals and sunny yellow centers, these delicate flowers evoke a sense of purity and childlike wonder. The daisy's association with innocence stems from its humble and unassuming nature, serving as a gentle reminder of the innate beauty and simplicity found in the world around us. It reminisces the early days of childhood and innocence.

FINE IS EVERYTHING

everything is fine.
fresh pancakes waft through the air
a smile of blueberries upon its face
I plunge a fork in.

the neighbor waters his lawn
green, lemony blades
the hose spraying specks over him.
everything is fine.

everything is fine.
kids crowd hallways
pushes and shoves cover me
I shove back.

My pizza slice cries grease
slippery fingers pick it up
it falls back down.
everything is fine.

everything is fine.
whispers follow me down the hall
like claws scratching down my back
scars reopen.

everything is fine.
everything is fine.
Fine is everything.

Credit: Anna Romanova/Pexels

Black dahlias embody a profound symbol of betrayal and sadness, exuding an aura of mystery and darkness. Unlike their vibrant counterparts, these flowers possess a unique allure that reflects the depths of human emotions. With their deep, velvety petals and somber beauty, black dahlias evoke a sense of heartbreak and the pain of betrayal. They serve as a poignant reminder of the complexities and sometimes painful realities of relationships.

FACE VALUE

One face.
kids run around me in a blur
crouched with a book in hand I sit
a tiny black dot in a sea of swirls

criss cross.criss cross.
students dart around
one approaches and asks a question
I lie.

Two faces.
I have a friend now
sure is swell
We both like the same things
if I keep inside

One more approaches
out of the blue
another question is asked
and I lie again too

Three faces.
"Why are you acting strange"
One friend asks
With a start
I remember that I put on the wrong mask.

New school, new me.
A whole group approaches
I lie once more
and they swallow me whole.

Ten faces.
I get along with everyone oh so well.
they all love me for who I am
So long as the faces...
they're kept apart.

Every day I crumble some more.
Questions chip at me piece by piece.
Rip.Rip.Rip.
And I am whole.

Credit: Cup of Couple/Pexels

Snapdragons are symbolic of deception, characterized by their captivating appearance and playful demeanor. These flowers, with their vibrant colors and distinctive shape resembling dragon heads, evoke a sense of intrigue and hidden intentions. Their unique ability to open and close when squeezed mimics the movement of a mouth, alluding to the concept of concealed motives and trickery. Snapdragons serve as a visual reminder of the masks people may wear and the potential for manipulation and deceit.

<u>WILT</u>

Was I too young?
When you threw insults of jagged glass
Carved sharp daggers of mediocrity my way
Squished a star into a box
for it was much too great
Made me feel like I was nothing
when I couldn't relate
Poisoning my roots until only a wilted flower remained!

Was I too young?
When my dreams were of the sun
a ray powering through and carrying me above
and so I grew and I grew
I grew some more for you
till I was too old for some and yet too new
The flower lost its petals
just as it began to bloom

Was I too young?
When I poured over grades
to fit with your jade
Obsessed over college
Ten years before the day
Stressed beyond the width of my age

Was I too young?
When you remarked on my weight
When you tore that little self-assurance and put it on a plate
When you bragged about thinness
And yet still complained
So I ate crumbs till I grew sick
Peeling off my weight
like slices of apples

Was I too young?
When you turned every doubt into reality
Every achievement into a regularity
Every flaw into a conversation
When you threw me in a corner
And left me to rot
Shadows coming at me from every way
"We always stick together", that's what they'd always say

Was I too young?
When you took this pity and turned it to rage
An angry little dot in a sea of gray
Whose only goals
were to gain your respect
I was so young when I met you!
And now it's like I've grown 4 decades
Plucked a young bloom's petals
Until it too looked slain

Was I too young-
I hate you
I hate you
I hate you
And yet the mere trace of your voices
throws me to my knees
Do you know what you did to me?
Do you care what you cost me?
Do you want to right the wrongs?
No.
But you still won't leave me be.

Credit: Credit: Ryutaro Tsukata/Pexels

Zinnias embody the symbolism of an absent and disappointing friend through their faded petals. These once vibrant flowers now bear the marks of neglect and indifference, reflecting the gradual decay of a friendship. The withering beauty of zinnias serves as a poignant reminder of the disappointment and hurt that can arise from a relationship that fails to provide the support and care it initially promised.

DAYDREAMS

I think I fell in love in May
But how can one be sure
———————————————

Does your heart pound from the tips of your toes-
to the wisps of your jet-black hair
Do you lift five fingers
Attempt a wave-
then run your fingers through a dark maze of curls

Does the beat of your heart crescendo
when the glimmers of your eyes meet
Does a breath of relief cry from you
every time it's them you see.

Does the entire room stop and stare
when the two of you enter
Light as a gossamer gown
swirling like egg yolk and paint

Does the thought of them make you giggle
Does the banter drive you home
Could strawberry tarts be sweeter
than their picture covered in dew

Do you picture them
when you clasp at your perfect future
Does the rain stop and shudder-
every time you walk close
If the world were to explode into a tiny dot
Would you still only think of them with you?
———————————————
No.
strange look
———————————————

Oh...okay
Flips to the next page of the book

Credit: Credit: Anastasia Prideina/Pexels

Carnations are renowned for their representation of devoted love, showcasing a delicate beauty and profound symbolism. These flowers have stood as timeless symbols of deep affection and unwavering loyalty, making them a cherished choice for expressing profound love and devotion. The gentle allure of their soft petals evokes a sense of tenderness and heartfelt affection, while the array of colors they come in carries nuanced meanings of love and admiration.

HAPPY POEMS

People say to write happy poems
Write about the sunshine and bluebells!
or perhaps a lovely mix
Write about moonlit dinners
or swirling in gossamer gowns
Perhaps a midday cheer
if that's your crowd

But what can one do if the rain is evermore?
If you can't stop your hand from falling
when you want to say hello
Ah yes a gossamer gown!
Only-
it's in a book
Moonlit dinners!
…next to my TV

You should write about the ocean
Mysterious and true
Or perhaps
Entering a quiet brick library
suitcase in one hand
Curling up with hot chocolate
When the thunder's so loud it shakes the bed

But what can one do if the ocean is just out of reach?
I can run and run eternally
But I'll still be ten feet deep
Oh to live in a library!
But with school-who has the time?
Hot chocolate and thunder shaking the bed?
California shakes its head

Oh to write happy poems!
To know and live the dream
But what can one do
Oh what should I do
If it's me, hiding in that fantasy

Credit: Credit: Karolina Grabowska/Pexels

Violets weave a tale of daydreaming through their enchanting and delicate presence. These captivating flowers, with their vibrant hues and ethereal fragrance, beckon us to delve into the realm of imagination and introspection. Violets are revered as gentle guardians of reverie, inspiring us to lose ourselves in thoughts and wanderings, embracing the beauty of quiet reflection and creative musings.

I

i'm a little stubborn
with a tendency to procrastinate
and a whole lot of irate

i'm a little spontaneous
yet driven to an end
might drive you up a wall
but always coax you down again

i'm a little bit ambitious
alright maybe a lot
i'd push a boulder up a mountain
to attain more than i've got

I'm a little curious
perhaps a bit much
reading books keeps me up past 3 am
just a touch

i like to think that i'm creative
but i'm running out of words
when it comes to me,
i is a difficult word

Credit: Pixabay/Pexels

Tulips embody the essence of creativity and expression, captivating us with their vibrant colors and graceful form. These exquisite flowers have been cherished as symbols of art and the unrestrained freedom of self-expression. From their diverse range of hues to their elegant and symmetrical petals, tulips awaken our imaginative spirits. Tulips serve as a reminder to nurture and celebrate the inherent creativity within, encouraging us to bloom with authenticity and artistic flair.

AFTERWORD

Hello again! Welcome back from your journey through these flowered pages of poetry. I hope you enjoyed the poems as much as I enjoyed writing them. I thought I would explain some of the highlights from the book, including the thoughts and stories behind my favorite poems:

Starting off strong we have *Sleepless Lament*. This poem serves as an ode to the late nights I've spent rethinking my actions of the day and of course, writing poems about them. It's safe to say that coffee is my best friend on the days following them!

One poem that doesn't quite fit in with the rest of the poems, also has unconventional inspiration. I wrote *Boo, Boombox* after watching a slew of 80s movies this past summer. Picturing myself in these movies, I was able to create an image through this poem. The last line "that's the only way you'd ever see me" is broader than the obvious meaning of being ignored by someone I'm crushing on. More so, it refers to how 80s movies always focus on a central character, and everyone always *sees them*.

Scram Sunny has an amusing backstory, much like the poem itself. I was initially planning to write an *aesthetic poem* about the "beautiful rays of sun" or something along those lines. Upon starting the poem, I realized that there were a lot more things I hated about the sun than admired on that particular day. And so, what started out as an ode to the sun, ended up being a satirical poem about avoiding opportunities for happiness.

The Cry Heard Around the World was actually the first poem I had written, outside of the daily poems with my teacher, after my brief writer's block. I have always deeply cared for the environment, but for some reason that one day the words just came to me. Allowing myself to be inspired instead of searching for inspiration was a big turning point in my poetry.

Among the entire chapter of Amor's Garden, *Fluffy Wings* remains the only poem that is even remotely true to my life. While the other poems held other sources of inspiration, this poem was inspired by my own life. The feeling of having a crush, only to have it be unrequited is represented through this poem, a feeling that many teens can relate to.

Oh so young is a poem that is especially important to me. Not only is it the first poem I had ever written, but it is also written about a particularly vulnerable part of my life. The actual poem itself lacks the complexities in pattern and style that my other poems have, but to this day it still remains the most raw and personal poem I've ever written, making it hold a very special place in my heart.

Speaking of raw and personal poems, *Face Value* is another one of my most genuine poems. The experience of feeling like you have to change yourself to fit in is one that many teens including myself could relate to. The unique structure was meant to resemble a snake, symbolizing the deception of pretending to be someone I'm not. Since then, I have thankfully learned to limit my *number of faces* but the poem is still one of the most relatable poems I've written.

Ah, the poem I was hesitant to write, yet compelled to do so—*Wilt*. Past friendships are always difficult topics to explore, and for me, *Wilt* was exceptionally difficult. This poem was about a past friend group I had when I was younger and the tremendous pressure and emotions I had because of them. The poem follows a traditional structure until the end when it breaks to express the true extent of my emotions at that time. Writing this poem was incredibly important because it served as a form of peace and closure for me.

Happy Poems was actually written after reading over all my other poems. When I realized that the vast majority of them were sad. At that moment, I made a conscious effort to write happy poems, but they simply eluded me. Thus, Happy Poems came to fruition, influenced by my tendency to excessively romanticize certain things, often overlooking the other sources of happiness in my life. It sheds light on the common phenomenon of people striving relentlessly for something, inadvertently disregarding the genuine blessings that surround them. It is also one of the closest my poems come to a "happy" poem!

Lastly, *I* is a reflection of myself as a person. I initially wanted to do a heartwarming and inspirational poem about self-exploration but I realized that even I don't know enough about myself to write that. Just as the poem states, "when it comes to me, I is a difficult word"; as a teenager, I feel immense pressure to define myself as a person, yet I'm merely skimming the surface of my own identity. This final poem brings the book to a close with a blend of wistfulness and hope, showcasing my best qualities while acknowledging the inherent uncertainty that accompanies my journey.

One thing is for certain though: poetry will be a part of my future. Thank you to my wonderful readers and I'll see you next time.

Signing off for now,

ABOUT THE AUTHOR

Hannah Mukhtar, a rising high school senior, has swiftly emerged as a passionate poet in just over a year. Growing up in California, she was immersed in the world of arts from an early age, with a particular inclination toward creative writing. Even as young as 6 and 8 years old, Hannah authored her first books, igniting her lifelong love for storytelling.

Her journey into poetry has been adorned with accolades, garnering multiple awards at the district and state levels. Notably, she clinched a prestigious 1st place honor from the California Federation of Chaparral Poets, showcasing her exceptional talent. As she looks ahead to graduation, Hannah envisions a path that merges her passion for economics with a pursuit of law.

Beyond the realm of poetry, Hannah's curiosity knows no bounds. She finds joy in exploring diverse realms, such as managing her e-commerce business on Depop (@moonzyhearts), founding the successful fundraiser Ramadan Bakery Boxes, and even delving into app development with her creation, Nutra, a current work in progress. Hannah's insatiable quest for knowledge extends to the intersection of two captivating subjects: fashion and economics, which she plans to explore further in an upcoming book.

For those intrigued by Hannah's poetry and eager to connect, she recently launched her poetry account, @mochapoetry. Feel free to explore her other social media platforms listed below for a deeper glimpse into her creative world.

Stay tuned for more captivating words and exciting endeavors from this blossoming young poet.